WHO IS JESUS

A MAN AND A GOD?

BY
GEM SCORP

Published by Hemingway Publishers
Cover Design by Hemingway Publishers
Isbn: Printed In The United States

HEMINGWAY
PUBLISHERS

DEDICATION

I strongly dedication this book this book the faithful followers of Christ. To the who believers and defenders of His deity. To those who are seeking the truth about Christ. And finally to those who believes in Him but doesn't accept His deity.

ACKNOWLEDGMENT

First of all, I would like to thank my God who gave me the courage to put my thoughts in writing. Since college days I wanted to write a book similar to this until finally things are now in print. Second, I would like to thank those individuals I had exchange of ideas since college days, including the different church leaders from different denominations whom I debated for years--- because of our different belief it lead me to this book. I would like to thank a friend in Philippines who is always willing to do the typing job for me even how bad my hand writing is. Finally, I will never miss to thank the love of my life whose presence gives me strength to continue my everyday battle.

CONTENTS

ABOUT THE AUTHOR

Gem Scorp is my American name but I already authored few other books under different screen names like **Poems for you** by Kuya Jap; **The Power of Fiction**; **The Journey** by Nitch Saver, and ofcourse my other book under Hemingway entitled **The 150 Psalms of Love and Poetry**. I'm a registered nurse by profession and use Christianity to extend the love of Christ in my nursing career. Through my different interactions with people, I develop a habit of reading and researching about the word of God. I keep my faith by serving in the Church of Christ and extend it through attending masses and classes in other church denomination in order to widen my understanding about the word of God and come up with my own. I'd been defending my faith since college days and attended as well several informal debates and forum about different views on the bible.

WHO IS JESUS?

For centuries, scholars, believers, and nonbelievers have been arguing about the nature and deity of Jesus.

Is he just a man? A God? A spirit? A small God?

Is He coming back? Is he the one riding on a white horse? Did Jesus build the church on earth? Who is Jesus for Muslims? Is Jesus, God the Father, and the Holy Spirit, are one and the same?

This book aims to enlighten the minds of the readers who are seeking the answers to the nature and deity of Jesus. This book will use simple analogy, analysis and understanding of the verses of the holy scriptures.

Let's get started!

JESUS AS A MAN

Jesus is fully human! He was born from a human mother (**Matthew 1:25**).

As a human, he was hungry (**Matthew 21:18**), and was thirsty (**John 19:28**).

He was not exempted from temptations (**Matthew 5:1**); he felt pain and suffered (**Matthew 16:21**);

And Jesus died (**Matthew 27:50**)

JESUS AS AN EXTRAORDINARY MAN

Yes, Jesus is fully human, but he is just extraordinary.

He was born to a human mother but a virgin (**Luke 1:27**).

Jesus was the only one born from a virgin human mother.

As a human, he got hungry and thirsty, but no human being can survive forty days and forty nights without food and water (**Matthew 4:2**).

He was tempted but overcame all his temptations (**Luke 4:1-13**).

He died like us, but he was risen on the third day (**1 Cor. 15:4**).

THE DIFFERENCE BETWEEN JESUS AND AN ORDINARY MAN

Jesus obeyed God until death (**Phil 2:8**) but man disobeyed God (**Rom 5:19**) (**Gen 3:12**)(**2 Cor 5:21; 1 Jn 3:5**).

Jesus has no sin (**2 Cor. 5:21; Hebrews 4:15**), while all men sin (**Rom 5:12-19**).

Jesus can love women (**Jn 8:10-11**) without lust (**Mt: 5:28**), but it is easy for a man to lust before loving a woman. (**2 Sam 11**).

Man was created to be married (**Gen 2:23-25; Jm 1:17**)

and has to be a husband of one wife if a man desires an office in the Church. (**1 Tim 3:1-7**).

But Jesus preferred not to marry (**1 Cor 7:8**).

Man needs to ask for forgiveness so that the heavenly Father can forgive him (**Mt 6:14**)

but Jesus can give absolutely pardon. (**Lk 5:20**)

if you want to follow him (**Luke 14:25-34**) and seek the kingdom of his Father (**Mt 6:33**).

WHERE WAS JESUS BEFORE HE WAS BORN?

We now have a background and understanding that Jesus is indeed a man, a human being. We previously pictured some qualities that made Jesus not just a man but an extraordinary man, and also, we showed that Jesus is somewhat different from an ordinary man.

The next question is: *who was Jesus before he was born*? Where did he come from? If he was born from a virgin, was he created?

The Son, Jesus, was in the bosom of the Father (**1 Jn 1:18**).

Our basis of understanding here is the Bible. The Bible clearly states that Jesus is in the bosom of the Father. The Bible did not mention that the Father implanted him or created him, but Jesus is in His bosom.

Next, since Jesus was in the bosom of the Father, then the Father gave birth to him (**Heb 1:5**). Did God create Jesus? *The Bible says, the Father gave birth to Jesus and it was never mentioned that Jesus was created.*

GOD THE FATHER CREATED JESUS

What did the Father mean when He said He gave birth to Jesus? It means Jesus was brought forth before God started to create heaven and earth (**Prov 8:22-28**).

Proverbs 8:27 says, "Jesus was there when God created the heavens. Jesus was there before any of the dust of the earth was made (Prov 8:26)."

If man was created from the dust of the earth (**Gen 2:7**), then definitely Jesus is not a man because Jesus already existed before the Father made the dust (earth).

11

WHERE WAS JESUS WHEN GOD CREATED HEAVEN & EARTH?

Jesus was at the Father's side (**Prov 8:30**).

We just found out that Jesus came from heaven, and he was not created, but God brought him out from His bosom.

Now, *who was Jesus before He was born*? Jesus is Lord (**Ps. 110:1**) even before the world existed (**Jn. 17:5**).

Take note here, that the Father called Jesus, Lord, in this passage. Thus, when Jesus, in human form, asked the Father to honor him to glorify, meaning to give him back the authority, Jesus voluntarily surrendered or renounced his godliness when he took the human form.

If we look at **Heb. 10:5-10,** Jesus came down to earth (meaning he was from heaven above) and took a human body that was prepared by His Father. He came to earth to obey the will of the Father.

Jesus, who is equal with God in being and in form (**Phil. 2:5-7**) chose to become like a man. *It is clear here that to become like a man means he was not a human being at first because he was equal to God in being and in form from the beginning.*

13

WAS JESUS CREATED?

Many believe that Jesus was created according to the scripture: **Colossians 1:15** (the firstborn of all creation). Take note of "the firstborn" of all the creations. It means he was there before all the created things (**Col 1:17**) because all things were created through Him (**Col 1:16**).

If we read **Jn 1:1-3**, it is very clear that Jesus was with God in the beginning, even before anything was created, and nothing will be made without him.

Was Jesus created? The answer is a NO.

IS JESUS A SMALL (MIGHTY) GOD?

We already learned that Jesus is a man and an extraordinary man. We just discovered too that Jesus was not created but a son of God the Father who was always with Him before the creation.

The next question is: Is Jesus a mighty God or, as others label him, "a small God?"

Let's examine how the Old Testament revealed Jesus Christ.

Isa. 9:6 revealed that Jesus Christ is a Mighty God. The psalmist agreed in **Ps. 95:37**, The Lord Jesus Christ is a mighty God. **Duet. 10:17** further explains it all that the Lord is God and a mighty God.

In the book of Revelation, Jesus claims that He is a Mighty God (**Rev. 1:8**), and John, who witnessed Jesus, revealed to us that Jesus is an Almighty God (**Rev. 4:8**).

IS JESUS A TRUE GOD?

Previously, we learned that Jesus is not only a Mighty God but Also an Almighty God.

Others may debate the claim that Jesus being in the "Almighty" is a leadership function just like a human king who is also a mighty King in power in ruling his subjects.

So perhaps, to better understand if Jesus is a mighty or Almighty God, it is better to discern first if Jesus is a True God.

Let's read **Jn 8:16**; in here, Jesus said He is not alone in making judgment, "but I and the Father."

In other words, *God the Father also does not decide alone, in a single word, "Jesus and the Father" decide as one.*

If Jesus is not a true God, why would the Father God (who is a true God) would consult?

JESUS HIS SON IN MAKING DECISIONS?

Does it make sense to all of us that a TRUE GOD will consult a man, a human being, in making His JUDGEMENTS?

If God knows everything (Ps 147:5; Jn 21:17; Heb 4:12-13; Jn 3:20), then why would God have to decide together with a man?

So, Jesus has to be a God also, Let's check again **Jn 1:1**… and the word was God.

In **Philip 2:6**, it was mentioned that Jesus "is in the very nature of God." We cannot remove the godliness of Jesus Christ because it is His very nature.

But what happened to Jesus Christ? Let's read **Phil. 2:7**. He removed His godly nature and took the nature of man. It's very clear that Jesus was not a man in the beginning because He took the form of a man. *If he was a man, does he need to take a human form?*

Common sense would say that in order to take a different form, there must be two different forms first.

IF JESUS IS A TRUE GOD, WHY PRAY?

Many believers nowadays are confused in the deity and nature of Christ. Perhaps of misunderstanding or being misinformed by some preachers or teachers who were not able to see the exact message of scripture.

Let's take **Jn 17:3,** for example. In here, the passage says, *"that they may know you, the only true God."* So many literally focus on this passage alone and conclude that Jesus is a man since Jesus himself explained to his followers that the Father is the only true God.

Is this passage correct? Yes! Absolutely correct. However, what is the picture in here?

Let's read the entire text; let's start from **Jn 17:1** - Jesus is praying here. Take note, we are talking about Jesus here, who came down from heaven **(Prov 3:4; Prov 8:26 - 30)** and took the form of a man **(Phil 2:7)**. Jesus directly removed his godly nature here, then he prayed.

Jesus (a man) was here on earth when he prayed to the Father in heaven. Obviously, He looked up to the Father and prayed and announced, "Father in heaven **(Mt 6:9-10)**, glorify your Son (man

23

on earth) and in **verse 3**, *Jesus announced that God the Father is a true God in heaven and who else? Jesus Christ also whom God sent. So, Jesus is a true God on earth.*

Why is Jesus a true God on earth (**Jn 17:3**)? Because there are many gods and lords on earth (**1 Cor. 8:5**).

If Jesus was a true God on earth when he was here, would God allow a man to be a god? Be worshiped?

WILL GOD ALLOW A MAN TO BE A GOD?

We know there is a True God. The question is, **can a true God make another god**? *Or can a true God make a man, God?* Let's read **Ex. 7:1**.

In here, God made Moses a god. Others may argue that Moses was not a true god. However, regardless of their doubts, the truth remains that a True God can make another god. *But when did the true God make something that is not real or fake*? Is there a verse that says a True God made up things? It would follow that this God is not true, a liar.

If God made Moses a god, how many gods are there?

HOW MANY GODS?

There are many!

Let's read **Ps 82:1**: God standeth in the congregation of the mighty, he judgeth among gods.

Take note of congregation, meaning an assembly, meaning there are many! Second, the verse mentions "mighty," which is why God is almighty; He is comparing himself to the other mighty gods.

Let's continue in **Ps 82:6**. God said, "You are gods," the children of the most high.

Many argue that these are false gods, but my question is: *who declared that they are gods*? Is it not God Himself who claimed that they are gods? Are the children of God, not true gods? I leave the answer to you, but I'll make a comment that if the son of man is a true human being, then it follows that the children of God are what???

Even Christ quoted this scripture in **Jn. 10:34-35**. Jesus is answering, *"You called me blasphemous when it is written that God called them gods? I'm a son of God, and I cannot be God?*

Do you notice that in **Gen. 1:26**, "Let us make man in our own image." God used the pronouns "us" and "our" because, in the beginning, there was more than one God.

DOES THE FATHER HONOR JESUS AS GOD ? (HEB, 1:8, ROM, 9:5)

I find it hard to believe that there are so many religious people at the present time who discredit the divinity of Christ, and yet we read the same Bible or scripture, which is the basis of our belief.

To end or settle this argument, if I can prove that the Almighty God called His Son "God," would this end the debate about Jesus as God vs. Jesus as only a man?

Let's read **Hebrews 1:8**. It is clearly stated that from this text that the Father called His Son "God." So, where did the disagreement come from?

I'm sure other religions will love to use the Lamsa translation of **Hebrews 1:8** which says, "Thy throne, O God, is forever and ever versus the traditional translation, which is "Thy throne, oh God, will last forever."

What's the difference between the two translations? It is clear that in the Lamsa's translation, it is not the son who is God but the "throne." Now let us put some sense in this claim. The Lamsa followers who love the Lamsa translation believe that there is only

ONE GOD, that Jesus is not God, and the Holy Spirit is not God. Now, *if the throne of God is the GOD*, the first question: **how many gods are still there**? The Father is God who is talking to the Son, and the "throne" is another god. Still, there are two gods in the picture, right? Second question: if indeed the throne of God is the "God" and Jesus is just a man, is it not very disrespectful of this translation to allow a man to sit on or over a God? I even handle my Bible with care and respect because I believe my Bible is a collection of the words of God.

Last question: if the throne of God is a "God," then it follows that anybody who sits on it can become a God. Then **John 1:18** will be correct in saying that Jesus is not a man because He is now seated on the throne of God.

Whatever translation you will use, it will still end up in proclaiming either Jesus as "a TRUE GOD" or "Jesus is not man but a God."

Let's take a look at another passage, and hopefully, this will convince you that, indeed, Jesus is God. **Romans 9:5**.

Is this passage clear enough, when it says, "Jesus who is over all God?"

But what kind of a god is Jesus?

AS A GOD, WHAT KIND IS JESUS?

Perhaps others will still find a way to say, "Yes, it is written that Jesus is God, but is it written that He is a true God? Where in the passage can you read the literal word "TRUE?"

This is another logic that others will use to misguide the believers. To answer this question, let's read again **Hebrews 1:8**. In this passage, it is God the Father who is talking, agree? If the Father God said that Jesus is God, if He is telling the truth or not? Where in the Bible says that God the Father does not tell the truth all the time?

If God the Father tells the truth all the time, then we cannot make His son a man when the Father calls Him as "God."

If we are now convinced that Jesus is a True God, are you still going to question: He is God but not the almighty? Or perhaps you will say, give me the passage that says Jesus is the Almighty God.

If I can give the passage that proclaims Jesus is the Almighty God, will you accept Jesus in your heart as your God?

First, let me ask you this, who is coming back, is it God the Father or Jesus Christ? We will ask the Bible, and the Bible says in **Revelation 1:7**, "He is coming with clouds, and everyone sees Him

31

including those who pierced Him." There's our clue over there, **"Those who pierced Him**."

The one who is coming back will never be the Father because:

Everyone will see Him. The Father is a spirit, man will never see Him.

He was never pierced. This leads to Christ who was pierced to death on the cross.

Let's read as well **Titus 2:13**, "glorious appearing of the Great God and Savior. Does this passage say that the Father and the Son will come back together? Again, man will never see the Father and He was never pierced (**Rev 1:7**).

And for the grand finale, **Revelation 4:8**, who is coming back? The Lord God Almighty?

We just found out that Jesus is coming back but He is not coming back as a man but a Great God and Savior (**Titus 2:14**) and as a Great God Almighty (**Rev 4:8**).

Shall we continue to disagree if Jesus is just a man versus a Great God Almighty?

IS JESUS, GOD, & THE HOLY SPIRIT ARE ONE & THE SAME?

Human as we are, we tend to be creative in our thinking and we love to disagree even though we can read from the scriptures the answers to our questions.

Previously, we discussed that Jesus was not created, He came from heaven, and we cited passages to prove that He is a great God Almighty. The next question is: Is Jesus, Father, and Holy Spirit one and the same?

First, I'm a person who wants to use my sense first before quoting and analyzing the scripture. I just discussed that the Father gave birth to Jesus. Can they be one and the same? If you put logic into it, use a little common sense, **can you give birth to yourself and later on talk to yourself and tell yourself, "Let's make man in our own image**?" It doesn't make sense right?

If it doesn't make sense in our human understanding, how much more for God?

To end this confusion, let's examine **Matthew 3:16-17**. This passage talks about the baptism of Christ and in here it was shown that the heavens were opened and the Spirit of God descending like a dove then a voice from heaven was speaking.

The picture depicts Jesus (Son of God), Spirit of God (dove), then a voice from God in heaven (The Father). This passage alone will tell us that Jesus, the Holy Spirit, and the Father are not one & the same.

If you are still not convinced then let's apply the principle of the Bible taught by Jesus Christ.

According to Jesus. The sender is greater than the one being sent. (**Jn. 13:16**). This proves that the Father is greater than the Son. Now Jesus can also send the Holy Spirit which means, by principle, Jesus is greater than the Holy Spirit. Let's read: **Jn. 14:26, Jn, 15:26, Jn. 16:7**.

We just proved in this discussion that the Father, the Son, and the Holy Spirit are **not one and the same.**

ONE GOD, THREE PERSONS.

The long debated ideology in the Bible is: One God, 3 persons (personas). The word trinity is never found in the Bible. It is never thought but the three persons of God exist: Father, Son, and the Holy Spirit. To start, let us understand some basic concepts.

Other religions believe in Oneness. *Meaning the Father (Creator God, Son, and Holy Spirit) are one and the same but just exist in different time periods.* I already disproved this in the previous chapters. I don't have to elaborate on this one.

The other interesting belief is the **ABSOLUTE ONE**: meaning there is only one God, so Jesus as the Son of God is not a god but a pure man, and the Holy Spirit is the God creator Himself. I partially discussed this in the previous chapters.

In the previous chapters, I had proven that the Holy Spirit is a different person since Jesus can send the Holy Spirit. *If Jesus is just a man & the Holy Spirit & God the Father are one, then why is Jesus able to send the Holy Spirit if the teaching of Jesus is: The master is greater than his servant? By applying this principle alone, we can agree that the Holy Spirit or the Spirit of God is not the same as God the Father.*

Before we move forward, I think it is good to teach basic Hebrew words that are being used in this discussion. The first Hebrew word "YACHID" which translates as ABSOLUTE ONE. The second Hebrew word is "ECHAD" which means composite one or unity. To simplify usage of the words let's take a simple example. If I say, there is a man in the room, it means there is absolutely only one man, no other person in the room. This is YACHID. If I say there is a family in the room, although I used the word "one" family it doesn't mean only one person but one family is composed of a father, mother, and a child or children. This is "ECHAD."

Let's take a very familiar verse from the Bible. **Deuteronomy 6:4**, "Hear oh Israel! Yahweh is our God, Yahweh is one (ECHAD). To those who are not familiar with the Hebrew text, they will understand this text literally that OUR GOD is absolutely only one. But as you can tell, the Hebrew word is "echad" which only means God the Father together with the Son, and Holy Spirit which I will elaborate more later.

The same "ECHAD" is used in the text **Genesis 2:24** (and they shall become one flesh). So here, the two persons, husband and wife became one (ECHAD) flesh but you don't count them as one person (YACHID).

Another Hebrew word that I want to share is the word EL which means "God" (singular) versus ELOHIM which means gods (plural).

In **Genesis 1:1**, it says: In the beginning "ELOHIM." If you read the book of Genesis in Hebrew translation, everything is ELOHIM, meaning there is one God (ECHAD) but he was not alone (ELOHIM).

God the Father or God the Creator was never alone from the beginning but co-exist with His Son (**Prov. 8:26-30**) and the Holy Spirit (**Gen. 1:2**).

The Spirit of God (Elohim), it didn't say "God the spirit." Let's take Genesis verse by verse.

Gen. 1:1, in the beginning Elohim (plural) created heaven and earth. God the Father created heaven and earth then **Gen. 1:2**, the Spirit of God (Holy Spirit) moved upon the surface of the waters.

Gen. 1:3, and Elohim said (word= Son) in **John 1:1** (in the beginning (**Gen. 1:1**) was the word (**Gen. 1:3**) **John 1:14** the word became flesh and dwelt among us. It is very clear that there is one (ECHAD) God that co-exist with the Son and Holy Spirit from the beginning.

As we continue in **Gen. 1: 26** "let us" make man in "our image." Here the plural noun "us" and "our" are being used.

No one should argue that God the Father was talking with the angels because mankind was never created in the image of angels. If God was talking to the angels and we were created in the image and likeness of angels then mankind right now should have wings (**Rev. 4:8**).

When the Bible says one God (ECHAD) it does not say absolute oneness (YACHID). But one God co-exist with His Son and Holy Spirit who have also a nature of goodness. Can God (EL) exist alone (YACHID)? The answer is clearly No.

Remember, Jesus is that Word of God; Jesus is the Power of God; Everything was created through Him. Meaning if God the Father wants to exercise His Power, He has to use His Word (Jesus) and when He wants to send help to mankind He sends the Holy Spirit.

In fact when God gave Power to Moses, God gave him a staff (**Exodus 7:10-12**); **Numbers 20:7-11**.

In these verses, Moses used his staff in performing miracles but when God created the heavens and earth, He used His word.

I'm hoping that I'm bringing clarity about the 3 persons (ELOHIM) in the Bible who act as One God (ECHAD).

The Father, Son, and Holy Spirit act as one, they decide as one, they consult each other and love mankind as a union of One GOd (**1 John 5:7**, these three are one).

DID GOD THE FATHER ABANDON CHRIST?

I just proved in the previous chapter that there is one God but co-exist with other persons that have the same nature of a god, and Jesus is one of the 3 persons of the True God.

Now if Jesus is God, why did God the Father abandon him on the cross? Let's read **Mt. 27:46**, "My God, My God, why have you forsaken me?" (Eli, Eli, lama sabachthani). Many scholars believed that **Mt. 27:46** was written in Aramaic versus Hebrew and Greek. Since the majority agreed that this text was written in Aramaic, I prefer to use the translation that was written by someone whose native tongue is Aramaic than someone who just studies the language.

According to George M. Lamsa, who was born in Bishu (Turkey), a native Aramaic speaker, **Mt. 27:46** is translated as,

"My God, My God, for this I was kept." or a better translation, "Eli, Eli, (my God, my God), lama (for this purpose), shbk (was I spared)."

And if **Mt. 27:46** was a quotation from **Psalm 22:1** (long argument), is not the point of view on this chapter. In this chapter, I just proved that there is a better translation that makes sense to the believers.

WHO IS JESUS TO THE MUSLIM?

According to the holy book of the Muslim (Quran), Jesus is Holy (**Surah 19:19**), a Messiah (**Surah 3:45**), and the word of Allah" (**Surah 3:39**) that was "cast down" to Mary (**Surah 4:171**).

Notice how the Quran agrees with **Heb. 10:5** that Jesus is not from the earth, rather Jesus was cast down (sent to) to earth (to Mary). This shows that Jesus originates from the heavens as previously discussed. The most stunning part is that t*he Muslims believe Jesus is the Word of God and in the Arabic grammar you can't separate the "word" from the creator,* meaning the words coming from my mouth is Me.

Therefore, for the Muslims, since Jesus is the word of Allah (God), you can't separate them; and they are interdependent. *If there is no creator, there is no word, if there is no word it could mean that the creator is: 1) silent, 2) can't speak (dumb).*

If Jesus is the word of Allah (God) and if we say God created Jesus 2,000 years ago, then what happened to God 2,000 years ago? Was God silent? Dumb? Dead? Since Jesus is the word of Allah (God) He co-exist with God (John 1:1 and John 1:14). As long as God speaks, Jesus exists and God the Father makes

41

Jesus divine and having the nature of God.

Is Jesus higher than Muhammad? According to the Quran, Muhammad sinned and had to seek forgiveness (**Surah 40:55, Surah 47:19, Surah 48:1-3**) while Jesus Is Holy (**Surah 19:19**) only given to God and not to Muhammad.

Can the Muslims trust the Bible?

Some Muslims believe that the Bible cannot be trusted because it is corrupted. However, their Quran proved otherwise. **Their Quran says: The Book of Moses, the Psalms, and the gospels were all given by God** (Surah 2:87, Surah 3:31, Surah 5:46).

IS THE BIBLE SILENT ABOUT JESUS WHEN HE WAS 13 YEARS OLD & MORE?

The Bible said that the law of the Lord is perfect **(Ps. 19:7)** and the scripture is sufficient to sanctify **(2 Tim. 3:16-17)**. If the Bible is complete, how come we couldn't find any record about

Jesus when he was 13 years old or so? Is this so? There are scholars who believe that the Bible was silent when Jesus was 13 years old and above. According to a few, Jesus went to China and learned from Confucius.

Let us examine the Bible and find out what happened when Jesus was 13 years old. In **John 7:15** it reads, "The Jews were amazed and asked, "How did this man get such learning without having been taught?""

As you can see, the Jews were so surprised at how Jesus was able to teach well when no one was teaching Him. This showed that the Jews knew that Jesus never went to school to be taught.

So what Jesus did when he was young? Read **Mark 6:3**, "Isn't this the son of Mary, the carpenter?" That's right! The Jews knew Jesus very well. The Jews watched him grow. The Jews saw him doing

43

carpentry with his father Joseph.

In other words, it is just like in our time when we know exactly what our neighbor is doing since we see them every day.

So what Jesus was doing before His ministry? He was doing carpentry! That's right! When he was 13 years old to around 30 years old, he was doing carpentry and never went to school. The Bible is not silent at all. We just need to understand it.

CAN GOD BE A MAN?

We learned that Jesus came from heaven, He was with the Father, God Creator, when God creates the heavens and earth. Then Jesus came to earth through a human body that was prepared by His Father.

After learning that Jesus Christ has a nature of God, equal to God in nature and form, He is the power of God, and together, Jesus and the Father make judgment together. Then this means that God can be a man? Let's read **Hosea 11:9**. So many religious groups who believe that there is only one God (Yachid) and who deny the deity of Christ love to quote Hosea 11:9 which says "for I AM GOD, and not MAN."

Examine the verse carefully. Thus **Hosea 11:9** explains *that God is one alone (Yachid) and no one else?* To answer this let's read **Hosea 11:8** which says, "How shall I give thee up, Ephraim?" Oh there you go..

To understand **Hosea 11:9** we must understand why God made such a statement and verse **8 of Hosea 1**1 explains it that Ephraim is a dear son of Israel (**Jeremiah 31:20**) so even when Ephraim turned away from God, God will remain loving to Ephraim and because He is a God and not a man, He will return to Ephraim with compassion and not with hatred.

45

God explains, if He was a man, God would return to Ephraim with hatred (just like how men react when someone hurts them) but He is a God, so God will not return with

anger nor destroy Ephraim despite its wickedness (Hosea 11:9a).

Can God be a man? Yes. He was manifested in the flesh (**1 Timothy 3:16**). Jesus is the image of the invisible God (Colosians 1:15) that's why Jesus speaks the truth when He claimed that "He who has seen me (visible) has seen the Father (invisible) **John 14:9**. So then, the disciples and followers heard the decisions of the invisible God through Jesus (**Jn. 14:10**. His son is a man).

Therefore, we can conclude that God can be a man through Jesus who took the form of a man.

WHO CAME FIRST ⊢ JESUS OR ABRAHAM?

After I discussed everything where Jesus came from, where Jesus was before God created the heavens and earth– we now know that Jesus came first. Did He really? If Jesus came first, is it logical to think that Abraham must have seen Him then? Jesus claimed that He came before Abraham as recorded in **John 8:57-58**, and the Jews were filled with disbelief. And because they couldn't accept what Jesus claimed, the Jews were trying to kill Jesus (**John 8:39**). When the Jews told Jesus that they were Abraham's children, Jesus challenged them, "Why are you (Jews) trying to kill me if you were children of Abraham? (**John 8:40**)."

According to Jesus, if the Jews were truly children of Abraham they should do what Abraham did.

What Abraham did to Jesus?

Abraham rejoiced in seeing the days of Jesus (**John 8:56**). A few lessons we can take from **John 8:56**. One, Jesus indeed came before Abraham. That's why Abraham saw His days and Abraham was glad to see the days of Jesus.

Two, Abraham had no intention of killing Jesus, thus Abraham's children should not kill Jesus. And third, Jesus is telling all of us, "Do not be afraid of those who kill the body but cannot kill the soul **(Mt. 10:28)**."

The Jews can kill Jesus as a man, but not the Jesus who came from heaven because the Jesus who came from heaven and now living inside Jesus, who is man, is a spirit **(1 Corinthians 15:45)**.

WHO BUILT THE CHURCH ON EARTH?

This is another question that most Christians still argue till these days: who built the church on earth?

There is only one passage in the Bible where Christ speaks about building a church and yet most Christians leaders couldn't agree on who really built the church?

First let's end the debate of the question who is the rock because—it is never Peter as what other Christians believe because clearly in 1 Corinthians 10:4 it says, "And all drank the same spiritual drink, for they were drinking from a spiritual rock which followed them; **and the rock was Christ.**"

Should we continue to debate on this one?

Now let's focus In *Matthew 16:18*, "And I tell you that you are Peter, and on this rock I will build my church, and the gates of Hades will not overcome it (NIV)."

Here, we can clearly see that Jesus is talking to Peter. It follows that Jesus is the first

person while Peter is the second person. Now follow me closely.

49

Remember that Jesus is the Rock so if He is talking to Peter and He is telling Peter that, "Hey Peter I'm the Rock." Then if Jesus will build a church on The Rock that is Himself, how should Jesus say it to Peter?

Is it not the proper way of stating it is, "Peter, upon me (the Rock), I will build my church." But Jesus did not say it that way! Why?

Let's examine some passages why Jesus did not say it so.

In John 12: 49 it says, "For I did not speak on my own, but the Father who sent me commanded me to say all that I have spoken (NIV)." Ah huh. Did you notice something??? Jesus said, he is not talking on his own but of who??? THE FATHER.

Let's go back to Matthew 16:18, "And I tell you that you are Peter, and on this rock (my son, Jesus) I will build my church...." Can you hear now the voice of God the Father speaking through Jesus?

We cannot just assume all of these without the basis of the Bible itself. Let's examine more passages to support this claim.

Let's read Deuteronomy 18:18-19, "*I will raise up for them a prophet like you* from among their fellow Israelites, and I will put my words in his mouth. He will tell them everything I command him. I myself will call to account anyone who does not listen to my words that the prophet speaks in my name (NIV)."

Who is this prophet?

Let's read Acts 3:22, "For Moses said, "The Lord your God will raise up for you a prophet like me from among your own people; you must listen to everything he tells you (NIV)." Then in Acts 3:20, "and that he may send the Messiah, who has been appointed for you—even Jesus (NIV)."

Well, Well, Well. I rest my case here. These passages were not written to be hidden but for us to discover and to understand.

May the Lord God add understanding to whosoever reads this article.

THE REVELATION

I would like to end my book by discussing an interesting verse in Revelation. It is beautiful to start a book from Genesis and end it in Revelation just how the holy Bible is arranged. I will only touch one specific verse in Revelation which for me a lot of scholars and preachers misinterpret it. I'm hoping my readers will follow along carefully since this is a very interesting verse.

Let's start!

In **Revelation 6:1-2**, who do you think is the rider that is mentioned in this verse? Let me guess, most answers are from scholars and preachers (I already talked to a number of preachers in person) and the common answer I got is: JESUS. Is it really Jesus? Let us examine it.

Revelation **chapter 6 verse one** opens with the line: I watched as the "Lamb" opened the first of the seven seals. Did you notice who opened the first seal? It's the lamb (**John 1:29**). I don't have to enumerate a handful of verses to prove that Jesus is the Lamb. *If Jesus is the lamb who opened the first seal then why would you (preachers, scholars) believe that the first rider is*

Jesus? Are you telling me that Jesus opened the first seal then he went inside and came back out riding on a white horse? Does it

53

make sense and logical to you? My common sense is telling

me that it is not Jesus. If it is not Jesus, then who?

Let's examine further.

Revelation **chapter six verse two continues**: a white horse, its rider held a BOW, he was given a CROWN, and he rode out as a CONQUEROR bent on a conquest. Now I put emphasis on: a bow, a crown and conqueror for a reason. My first challenge question is, if this is Christ, does Jesus come as a conqueror or will Jesus come back as a Savior? A Judge? But a conqueror?

Conqueror means to conquer, to gain control through force like in a war. *Will Jesus come back and start a war?* Think. If you think that Jesus will not start a war, then he is not the conqueror in this text.

Next emphasis: A Bow. Will Jesus use a bow? In **Rev. 19:15**, Jesus will use a sharp sword. Next emphasis: A crown. Will Jesus be given a crown? In **Revelation 19:12**, "And on His head are many crowns."

I just laid down the reasons why **Rev. chapter 6:1-2** is not talking about Christ as I contrasted it with **Rev. 19:12-16**. Now, others will still insist that **Rev. 6:1-2** is Jesus. If the first rider is indeed Jesus, then how come all the four horsemen are bringing disasters?

See the following: **Rev. 6:4**, a red horseman who will promote war. **Rev. 6:5**, a blade horseman who will bring lots of suffering. **Rev. 6:7**, a pale horseman, who will bring death. As you can see, after the first seal was opened, the first rider on white horse were followed by four other horsemen in different colors and yet in **Revelation 19:14**, the white horse, whose rider is called Faithful and True (**Rev. 19:11**), the armies of heaven were following him (the white horse in Rev.

19:11) riding on white horses. Do you see the difference? The white horse in Revelation chapter 6 was followed by 4 horsemen in different colors while the white horsemen in Rev. 19 was followed by armies in heaven riding on white horses. White horses only.

Who is the white horseman in Rev. 19? *This is Jesus. Rev. 19:13, "His name is the word of God (John 1:1)." If the white horseman in Rev. 19 is Jesus, then who is the white horseman in Revelation chapter 6?*

Matthew answered who is the white horseman in Revelation chapter 6 and he is the Anti Christ (**Mt. 24:5**) and will deceive many just how many religions preached that **Rev. 6:1-2** talks about Jesus.

Mt. 24:6 continued: you will hear of wars (red horseman). **Mt. 24:7** there will be famines (black horseman) and if there will be famines then death follows (pale horseman). Now it is clear that Rev. 6:1-2 refers to the Anti Christ and not Jesus Christ.

To end my book, I would like to touch about the colors of the horses in chapter 6. You may not agree with me but just to tickle some curiosities in your head.

Chapter 6 of Revelation mentioned 4 colors: white, red, black, and green. Don't get confused, pale in Greek is "chlous" which is greenish or green.

Now which countries have colors white, green, red, and black on their flags? We have a few, Egypt, Yemen, Iraq, Jordan, Palestine, Syria, Kuwait, Sudan, UAE, etc.

What do you observe in these countries? What do these countries have in common? What do they love to do? I leave that for you to answer.

Final question on this chapter: What RELIGION has a flag with green, white, red, and black colors? Or whose church leaders wear green, white, red, and black colors?

SUMMARY

This book is discussing One True God (Echad) who created heaven and earth together with the

Son of God and the Spirit of God. This book further talks about how Jesus, a true God, from heaven who came to earth to take a human form to save humanity and how Jesus was

received by both Muslims and Christians.

Finally, this book deals with other issues that most Christians cannot agree on including the

book of Revelation.

www.ingramcontent.com/pod-product-compliance
Lightning Source LLC
Chambersburg PA
CBHW051553120626
46551CB00013B/1503